www.finishinglinepress.com

Hey, Yard Duty, Johnny Said the "F" Word

poems by

Kevin Neill Gunn

Finishing Line Press
Georgetown, Kentucky

Hey, Yard Duty, Johnny Said the "F" Word

Copyright © 2016 by Kevin Neill Gunn
ISBN 978-1-944251-90-1 First Edition
All rights reserved under International and Pan-American Copyright Conventions.
No part of this book may be reproduced in any manner whatsoever without written
permission from the publisher, except in the case of brief quotations embodied in
critical articles and reviews.

ACKNOWLEDGMENTS

Peanut Butter   "Song of the San Joaquin" Spring 2009

Editor: Christen Kincaid

Cover Photot: Connie Post.

Author Photo: Connie Post

Cover Design: David Alpaugh

Printed in the USA on acid-free paper.
Order online: www.finishinglinepress.com
          also available on amazon.com

Author inquiries and mail orders:
Finishing Line Press
P. O. Box 1626
Georgetown, Kentucky 40324
U. S. A.

Table of Contents

*Thanks to my mom for inspiring the title
and to my wife Connie Post
for mentoring me with my first book*

Peanut Butter

some students
stick to the roof of my mouth
like peanut butter
their unpalatable presence
spreads over the classroom
with thick remarks
I find difficult to swallow

Anybody . . .?

I ask the class a question
wait for a response
the seconds calendar over me
like the month of January
nothing
not one student has anything to say
I rephrase
thinking they don't understand
still not a stir
I attempt to stimulate a discussion
clarify what I mean
offer an illustration
the lesson glaciers along
I look at the clock
pray for a thaw
only five minutes have passed
feels like an eternity
to a teacher on ice

First Day Of Class

students uneasy their way
into my classroom
study me at the podium
stares intersect
dissect
the awkwardness
impressions read volumes
measure expressions
gauge glances
expectations
plead on appearances
anticipation begs

I teach history
but chemistry is my concern

Seating Chart

names
personalities
aptitudes
dynamics
learning styles
attitudes
reduced to this piece of paper
I crumple to throw away
I discard the family atmosphere
I worked so hard to build
prepare to write down the names
of incoming islands of dysfunction

First Five Minutes of Class

students orbit my podium
I feel the magnetic pull
of their needs
my hemispheres circumscribed
by their demands
tardy slips
parent notes
field trip forms
shower me like meteors
absentees gravitate toward me
like asteroids on a collision course
with the end of the semester
I explore the black hole
of my file cabinet
for make up work
check the constellations
on my seating chart
pass back homework
attempt to bring order
to my second period
solar system

Tardies

excuses
dressed in denial
arrive on skateboards
mock punctuality
parade lame logic
past my skepticism
park their irresponsibility
next to my consternation
open their backpacks
brimming with disregard
and disruption

Onions

I grow onions in class
multi-layered lessons
I feed my students
I labor to teach them
to peel back the outer skin
inhale the information
sniff through the sources
analyze the aroma
breathe deeper
uncover the pungent odor
of insight
a smell that will stay with them

Pied Piper

they cling to cliffs
in the back of the classroom
lofty
aloof
afraid to let go of themselves

I try to lure them closer
to the ledge
entice them to take in the view
of what they can learn
what they can become

the task is steep
to coax their enthusiasm
off the precipice of participation
get them to trust
that I will honor
their free fall

"Hey, Yard Duty . . .!"

"Hey, Yard Duty!"
Johnny said the "F" word
"No I didn't,
you're a nerd"

recess at elementary school
like a circus,
that's the rule
high wire act on monkey bars
full of showoffs,
would be stars
children hang at every angle
upside down,
their stomachs dangle
on the playground
clowns at play
a belching, farting cabaret
playmates argue
the same old song
who is right
and who is wrong
teacher tries to arbitrate
yells at kids who roller skate
four-square follies
chase down balls
hyper kids
bounce off the walls
the midday mayhem
recess brings
until the bell
in mercy rings

RIP

a quiet class
is easy to manage
but so is a cemetery

students sit and stare
like sphinxes
their silence settles over me
buries my enthusiasm
dulls the sharp edges of my wit
turns me into a caretaker
of this first period mausoleum
the grim reaper of conversation
visits his death knell
on class discussion
may it rest in peace

On Being Boring

monotone drone
heavies the collective consciousness
dulls the wits
weights the desk
where snoring student
sits

words dispensed
like sleeping pills
somnolent statements
dry as the chalkdust
smudged on slacks
a yawn distracts

students slouch
hang eyelids at half mast
mourn the lingering death
of learning

Hormones Ahoy

middle-school madness
a daily kinetic energy symposium
hormones hightailing at warp speed
personal space invaders
on a mission
overtouching
in your face
a crude cacophony
of bodily sounds
manners held hostage
boys and girls
repel and attract
guided by a force field
they don't understand

teachers are ringmasters
as they reign in
these pre-adolescent performers
bring order to the awkwardness
and attempt to choreograph
this eighth grade circus

Cafeteria

the arena
where grub gladiators clash
face off in food fighting freeforalls
an institutional fraternity
of fastfoodaholics
daily pledging
complex carbohydrates
cookies
candy
pizza
chips
french fries
burritos
and chicken strips
they eat in a flash
leave the trash
with skill and precision
as if by instinct
not some conscious decision
supervisors try to make them be cleaner
but alas
they labor against nature
their efforts are in vain
against this hit and run hurricane

Homework Hieroglyphics

words obscured
by penmanship
migraine my brain
lightly shaded pencil
pushes the envelope
of extrapolation
to the limit

a closet cryptologist
I examine the context
search for clues
hum the "I hate to grade papers"
blues
decode
decipher
the shrouded syntax
declare the enigmatic answer
MIA

Tightrope

I walk the tightrope
every day in class
feel netless
inch my lesson plans
out into the arena
where spectators await
my performance
it can be a tough crowd
the trick is to teach them
to be participants
without losing control of the show
it's all about balance
I teeter at times
try to focus on where I want
to take the audience
how I hope to school them
intercom announcements
rattle my equilibrium
rude remarks try to sabotage my steps
I wobble
try not to lose my composure
summon my experience
lean on my lesson
to help me
stay the course
finish my act

the audience exits
I sit down at my desk
prepare for tomorrow's show

Wired

my students are wired
to many things
makes it hard for me to compete
cd players
and portable Gameboys
iPods
smartphones
and other high tech toys

some students
are wired by nature
their chromosomes plug them in
or so they claim
these Ritalin renegades
have their medication
and ADHD to blame

sugar charges kids batteries
frappuccino
candy sales
too much Captain Crunch
soft drinks
turn kids into kites
they fly in after lunch

other kids
hook up to drugs
call it meth
call it crank
these off the wall space cadets
always find a piece of my chain
to yank

the worst go wireless
they treat their cellphones
like umbilical cords
keeps them in touch with everything
but learning
they can even talk without a voice
text messaging
their designer distraction
of choice

I wish my students
were more connected
and a lot less wired
vying for their attention
makes this teacher
tired

Classroom Cacophony

candy wrapper crinkling conspirators
unwrap my concentration
chronic pen clickers
finger frustration
spiral notebook tearing
puts me on edge
moves my sanity
closer to the ledge
students rummage
through backpacks
and purses
cannot hear
my clandestine curses
gum chewing collaborators
smack and pop
someone help me
make it stop
cellphones
are the final straw
reserve a place
inside my craw
little noises
infiltrate
gnaw my nerves
irritate
sidetrack me
when I'm on stage
stir a homicidal rage
I wish I could
just ignore it
my stress would be
much better for it

Angler

I'm going fishing
hoping to catch my limit
did I choose the right bait?
will my students be biting?
can I hook their attention?
I trawl the classroom
trying to get to a deeper level
of understanding
that's where the real beauties are
insights feed near the bottom
I cast my questions
a student hits the line
I reel in the answer
not bad
I change lures
offer points for class participation
angle the discussion
throw back insignificant comments
pull out observations
weigh conclusions
measure meaning
many keepers

what a great day to fish

Ghosts

are in my classroom
they stealth through each semester
slipping between the cracks
of the curriculum
they are quiet
polite
never ask any questions
try to blend in
sitting in the back
I lose track
focus on larger than life
disrupters

the ghosts
are there every day
their low maintenance
makes them invisible
they are like the ocean
at low tide
leaving only scant signatures
on my Socratic sands
the computer brings them
into view
whenever progress reports
or grades are due

The Duck Hunter

homework is due
excuses lame duck their way
around my desk
each wonders if their story
will fly
I shoot most down
others never get off the ground

The Fireman

I stand at the podium
survey the scene
see some possible hot spots
two highly combustible corners
of the classroom
I launch my lecture
it soars high over the heads
of my students
I turn my back
to write on the board
hear one corner ignite
whispers
laughter
not exactly what I'm after
I try to extinguish the sparks
douse their rude remarks
with a not so tepid tirade
spray sarcasm in the direction
of the oral arsonists
my temperature rises
I tell them not to talk
check the clock
twenty minutes to burn

Sergeant Spitball

some classes
bring out the military in me
I soldier my commitment
to classroom control
plan tactics to subdue my students'
weapons of mass disruption
fill out discipline referrals in triplicate
for key insurgents
pre-emptive strikes
like changing my seating chart
contacting parents
have failed to undermine
my adversaries
these sabotage specialists
employ guerilla warfare
turn my room into
a minefield of mischief
I hunker down behind my podium
rally all my reserve
prepare to lead my lesson to the front
wishing I could call in the marines

What's The Point?

I endeavor to enlighten my students
empower them to think and express themselves
grow them towards discovery, self-awareness
and a wider world view
yet
paper airplanes found on the floor after class
notes passed between students during lecture
drawings on desktops
a machinegunsworth of putdowns
and other rude remarks
deloft my noble objectives
subvert the sacredness of my calling
reduce the romanticism of education
into a pedestrian parlor game
a no-holds-barred immaturityfest
in which I am the referee
yet
sometimes a student stays after class
asks me questions
shows some interest in what we are studying
thanks me for helping them understand

and I remember

Mr. Inspiration

standing in front
as always
struggling to inspire
somehow generate some enthusiasm
spark some ember of marginal interest
I look out at blank expressions
staring back at me
with ironclad eyelids
my students
mesmerized
anesthetized
catatonic
I feel like the curator
of a wax museum
masquerading as a history teacher

can I really be this boring?

apparently so, Shaundra's snoring

Five Minutes Left

crunch time
time to pull the pieces
of the lesson together
clarify
make connections
draw conclusions
fend off unwanted intrusions
announcements intercom
their attention stealing way
into these critical moments
I watch my students' fleeting focus
evaporate
like flatulence in a space suit
backpacks open
textbooks close
I plow ahead
raise my voice
refuse to wave the white flag
yet feel like Custer

The End of Class

students crowd around the door
jockey for position
"can we leave early?"
"not yet"
I feel relieved
the class is almost over
I worry I forgot to say something significant
something that might leave a lasting impression
what will they take with them when the bell rings
besides backpacks
wisecracks
and loads and loads of historical facts

did I do enough to reach them?
did I get through their cd players and cellphones?
did I touch them in any way?
what exactly did they learn?
I bite into my apple
and chew on my concern

Overboard

"help me,
I'm drowning"
"I'm in over my head"
"throw me a lifeline"

students splash
struggle to stay afloat
somehow during the semester
they missed the boat

caught in the current
they swim upstream
beg for mercy
try to redeem

they see their grade sinking
they flounder and flail
ask what they can do
so they won't fail

I could play the lifeguard
come to their aid
extra credit is buoyant
it could rescue their grade

if they paid more attention
when work was assigned
then they'd be on board
and not left behind

I could go in the water
or stay dry instead
I think I'll watch closely
see how long they can tread

Let the Begging Begin

"I turned that in"
"I know I did that"
"you must have lost my assignment"
"I'm this close to an A"

grades are due
that's their cue
to beg and whine
plead their case
manufacture mercy
if they can
work me
angle me
that's the plan

I add up points
factor in attendance
participation
place my faith
in the almighty computer
as percentages
parcel out penance

judgment day
in room P-14

Amnesia

I walk down the supermarket aisle
look up
notice someone approaching
"Hi, Mr. Gunn,
remember me?"
"I had you for History
back in '93"
I smile
nod
"it's nice to see you
how are you doing?"
her name
all the while
I am frantically pursuing
not Becky
not Jennifer
not Michelle
or Marianne
not Amanda
or Sarah
I know it's not Leanne
she studies my expression
my silence un-acknowledges her
she thought she had made an impression
I give her a hug
say, "take care"
feel bad inside
I couldn't recall her name
no matter how hard I tried
she put on a brave face
acted like she didn't notice my omission
but it hung over our conversation
and followed me home that night
I take pride in remembering my student's names
it lets them know they mattered
she did

Kevin Gunn has served as poet laureate of Livermore from 2013 until 2014 and has been asked by the city to continue in his current position until 2016. During his first term as poet laureate he started a highly successful program called Teen Poet of the Month to showcase the poetry of local high school poets. Kevin continues to curate the longstanding Ravenswood poetry series in Livermore. He also started an open mic poetry event under the oaks at Alden Lane nursery. In Kevin's second term he taught poetry lessons in eight of Livermore's elementary schools, focusing primarily on third and fourth grade students. He has written a number of poems for the city of Livermore to help celebrate community events.

Kevin taught history at Livermore High School for thirty nine years, retiring in 2014. While at Livermore High he started a poetry club that met once a week for over twenty years. Kevin has written hundreds of poems during his tenure at Livermore High for retiring faculty members, graduation ceremonies and other school events. He has served as judge for several local poetry contests including the Alameda County Fair. Kevin has appeared on a poetry TV show with his poet wife, Connie Post.

Kevin has won awards in the Las Positas annual poetry contest, the Alameda County Fair and Ina Coolbrith's poet's dinner contest. His poems have been published in the Chiron Review, Song of the San Joaquin, the California Quarterly, and many local community college anthologies.

www.ingramcontent.com/pod-product-compliance
Lightning Source LLC
LaVergne TN
LVHW091234080426
835509LV00009B/1280

* 9 7 8 1 9 4 4 2 5 1 9 0 1 *